Ten
tough
things

A bold plunge into the Christian life

Group
Incredible things will happen®

Loveland, Colorado
group.com

Group resources actually work!

This Group resource incorporates our R.E.A.L. approach to ministry. It reinforces a growing friendship with Jesus, encourages long-term learning, and results in life transformation, because it's

Relational
Learner-to-learner interaction enhances learning and builds Christian friendships.

Experiential
What learners experience through discussion and action sticks with them up to 9 times longer than what they simply hear or read.

Applicable
The aim of Christian education is to equip learners to be both hearers and doers of God's Word.

Learner-based
Learners understand and retain more when the learning process takes into consideration how they learn best.

Visit our website: **group.com**

Credits
Senior Editor: Candace McMahan
Editor: Stephanie Dyslin Martin
Chief Creative Officer: Joani Schultz
Copy Editor: Janis Sampson
Art Director: Jeff A. Storm
Cover Designer: Jeff A. Storm
Book Designer/Print Production Artist: Bob Bubnis
Production Manager: DeAnne Lear
Unless otherwise noted, Scripture taken from the HOLY BIBLE, NEW INTERNATIONAL VERSION®. Copyright 1973, 1978, 1984 by International Bible Society. Used by permission of Zondervan Publishing House. All rights reserved.

ISBN: 978-0-7644-3896-7

10 9 8 7 6 5 4 3 2 1   18 17 16 15 14 13 12 11 10 09

Printed in the United States of America.

CONTENTS

Foreword by Alex and Brett Harris 4

Introduction 6

Mapping the Adventure 8

Tough Thing #1   **Get Off the Sidelines** 11

Tough Thing #2   **Deny Yourself** 21

Tough Thing #3   **Passionately Pursue** 29

Tough Thing #4   **Become a Disciple (Part 1)** 35

Tough Thing #5   **Become a Disciple (Part 2)** 43

Tough Thing #6   **Defend Your Faith** 49

Tough Thing #7   **Share Your Faith** 59

Tough Thing #8   **Act Shrewdly** 65

Tough Thing #9   **Love Your Enemies** 73

Tough Thing #10 **Do Justice** 81

FOREWORD

ALEX and BRETT HARRIS

We were 16 when we started calling other teenagers to join us in choosing to rebel against low expectations and do hard things for the glory of God. The response has blown us away. Teenagers today want to be challenged. They need to be respected. They're not stupid. And they're frustrated when people don't expect them to understand or care about things that actually matter. What's more, they're starting to realize that God wants to use them right now, as teenagers—they don't have to wait!

In the past three years we've come across countless young people who are changing the world for Christ. These are young people who were 12 when they began to hate slavery, 14 when they had compassion on the homeless, or 16 when they decided that bringing clean water and the gospel to Sudan was not impossible. These are young people who are reaching for more, doing hard things, and raising the bar.

In 1 Timothy 4:12 the Apostle Paul not only commands young people to reject a culture that looks down on them because they're young, but he also challenges them to be examples to fellow believers in every area of their Christian lives. We see our peers grabbing hold of that high standard, taking responsibility to do, to act, and to lead.

But teenagers aren't the only ones who are waking up to what God is doing. Rick Lawrence is one of many leaders who have recognized that teenagers are tired of being labeled "good kids" for all the bad stuff they don't do—that they want to be known for what they *do*. Rick realizes that teenagers are ready for youth group to be more than a place to go on Wednesday night for a funny skit, a slice of pizza, and a Bible verse. And he understands that teenagers need mentors who will challenge them to reach their full, God-given potential.

By writing this set of small-group studies, *10 Tough Things*, Rick has done a tremendous service to the body of Christ—not just for youth pastors and leaders, but for teenagers themselves. This 10-week series is not about keeping your youth occupied and entertained. It's about equipping them and sending them out. It won't keep them out of trouble, but it just might get them into the right kind of trouble—the kind that comes when a young person steps up to the challenge to trust God, dream big, and do hard things for Christ.

Twin brothers Alex and Brett Harris are the founders of TheRebelution.com and bestselling authors of Do Hard Things: A Teenage Rebellion Against Low Expectations *(Multnomah Books). Based in Portland, Oregon, they are currently freshmen at Patrick Henry College in Purcellville, Virginia.*

INTRODUCTION

RICK LAWRENCE

I started thinking about creating this 10-week study after I read Alex and Brett Harris' culture-changing book, *Do Hard Things*. The book's message has already resonated so deeply with a vast army of teenagers. The tagline says it all: "A teenage rebellion against low expectations." Alex and Brett didn't start this rebellion, but they've done a great job of naming it and fueling it.

Aside from how their book has personally influenced me, I think the Harris brothers have tapped into a huge undercurrent in teenage culture. I know from personal experience that so many teenagers are tired of the missionless life they've been handed by adults, and they're hungering for something more...something hard-but-good. If you're a teenager reading this, maybe that describes you. I know that, because of this hunger, I feel a greater sense of kindred spirit with today's teenagers than I've felt at any time during the last two decades of serving as editor of Group Magazine (the world's most popular youth ministry resource).

Teenagers want more, and I want more.

More of Jesus.

More of the "fully alive" life that St. Irenaeus was targeting when he wrote, "The glory of God is man fully alive."

And so I felt a momentum building in me to respond to what *Do Hard Things* stirred in me, and what it's stirring in the hearts of teenagers. These Bible studies are geared for hungry people and for people who don't know they're hungry but really are. I've led portions of all of them in a variety of settings—small groups, retreats, Sunday school, and larger gatherings.

Although these studies have no direct connection to Alex and Brett's book, they're "swimming in the same pool" in that they ask something of you. The expectations are set high, not low.

The studies are based on these premises:

- Teenagers are smart, insightful people who can see and embrace deep truths.
- Teenagers like to explore things in the context of relationships.
- Teenagers are willing to try new things and experiment with new ways of learning.
- Teenagers want to feel respected. They're drawn to things that are challenging and demanding.
- Teenagers want to have fun—to feel fully engaged—when they're exploring the Christian life.

If I were standing in front of you right now, I'd have a big smile on my face and a look of excitement in my eyes. It's the same look you have before you get on a roller coaster or go bungee jumping... or pray as someone commits his or her life to Christ. So thank you. Thank you for taking a risk and taking a plunge into something that will change your life. I'm diving with you.

Mapping the Adventure

Here's a quick overview of what you can expect as you launch this journey:

1. The studies are designed so anyone—adult or teenager—can lead the group through them. Everyone in your small group or class needs a book, but anyone can lead. It's best to choose someone in advance to be the leader of each study, because sometimes there are a few things to gather in advance of the study. But as long as you have the supplies gathered in advance, anyone in the group—adult or teenager—can lead. You can assign someone to lead each study, or different people in the group can lead different portions of each study.

2. The instructions for these studies make leading a snap. The designated leader will need to do a little advance preparation but not much. Usually, it just means renting a DVD or gathering a few basic supplies. If you're leading one of these studies, pay close attention to the instructions so you can easily give them to everyone. Also, I often lead people into experiences or conversations by asking everyone to just "play with it." I often catch myself saying something such as "There's nothing on the line here. We're just going to experiment, and I'd love for you to just go with it." This gives people permission to be uncomfortable but clearly communicates that you won't give them an "out." If you're a teenager leading these studies, don't be afraid to simply read some of the stuff you're supposed to say. Follow the instructions, and you'll quickly feel comfortable leading. A lot of what you'll be doing is simply asking good questions.

3. These 10 studies have a progression to them, but it's loose (except for the two studies on becoming a disciple). Feel free to mix up the order of the studies if you want or to skip one if you need to. The topics aren't "siloed." They overlap with each other all the time and even reference each other. I'm merely separating them for the sake of focus.

4. The studies use a variety of methods to engage people, moving them from mere listeners to full participants. You'll enjoy learning by using film, experiences, great conversations, and group explorations. Some studies have almost no preparation; some require that you find and cue up a film clip or gather a few easily found supplies. The key thing is to enter into these studies with an attitude of curiosity and adventure—the kind of attitude that says, "Let's just try it!"

5. The studies use a fun, engaging learning strategy. You won't find lectures or fill-in-the-blanks—strategies that have questionable long-term impact on participants. In a typical small-group Bible study or Sunday school class, the leader talks most of the time. Sometimes a couple of discussion questions get tossed out, but often they're only a side dish to the real meat of the study. In this series, *everyone* talks. A lot. If you're leading one of these studies, you'll feel more like a ringmaster than a lecturer. That's good because research shows that people learn best by *doing*. In fact, the people who learn the most in any class are the teachers because they have to "own" what they're teaching.

6. Many of these studies include experiences that you'll do and then "debrief." By "experiences," I mean activities that require everyone to participate, not just sit back and listen. These might be fun, meditative, or mildly uncomfortable. But the goal is to plunge into activities that make you feel fully engaged. Debriefing is just another way of saying that you'll talk about how the experience affected you.

7. Bring a Bible with you to these studies. And bring extras, if you have them, for people who forget to bring one.

8. Finally, the best "supply" you can bring to this study is your own curiosity. I believe these studies will change and deepen the way you live your life and will draw you closer to Jesus. Thanks for having the courage to dive in.

Tough Thing   No. 1

GET OFF THE SIDELINES

Study Prep

The point of this study is to help people experience the difference between a life lived on the sidelines where it's "safe" and a life lived on the playing field where everything we are and do matters. Jesus is inviting teenagers to join him on his "grand adventure"— to leave the sidelines and get out on the playing field with him. If we're going to live in the adventure that Jesus has reserved for each of us, we'll have to lose our lives in order to find them (see Matthew 16:25). That's a tough but good thing.

Note on Supplies

You'll need a DVD of the film *The Lord of the Rings: The Return of the King* (extended edition).

Video Clip

To begin, play the "Coming Home" scene from *The Return of the King*, the last film of *The Lord of the Rings* trilogy. Cue up the extended edition of the film to Side B 1:40:10, and play the clip until 1:41:41. The scene opens with Frodo narrating the four hobbits' journey home and ends after Sam leaves the table to talk with Rosie.

After the clip, someone should say: The background of this scene from the last film of *The Lord of the Rings* trilogy is pretty simple. It's the aftermath of one of the grandest adventure stories ever written or filmed. In this scene, the four hobbits return home to the Shire after helping save the world from an overwhelming evil. They left home as immature boys whose main occupation was getting into trouble and drinking beer. They returned as seasoned warriors who'd experienced more terror and triumph than their whole village put together. In a bit, we'll look at this scene again, but a lot more closely.

Partner Talk: *(2 minutes)* Get together with a partner, and discuss these questions for two minutes or so:

- What's the greatest adventure you've had in your life? What exactly made it an adventure?

After two minutes, get back together as a group.

Someone should say: Call out some specific words (at least 10) that describe adventures. Everyone should record the words in his or her book.

1.	6.
2.	7.
3.	8.
4.	9.
5.	10.

Someone should say: It's interesting that not all our words are "happy" words. Some are difficult or even scary words (for example, *risky* or *dangerous* or *unknown*).

Someone should ask: *(5 minutes)*

- What makes an adventure "exciting" or "exhilarating"?
- If there's no possibility of danger, can something still be an adventure? Why or why not?
- If there's no challenge to overcome, can something still be an adventure? Why or why not?

- What are some of the differences between being in an adventure and being an observer of someone else's adventure?

Someone should say: It's one thing to watch or read about an adventure like *The Lord of the Rings*, but it's another thing to actually be *part* of such a grand adventure. When Jesus invites us to join his family by committing our lives to him, he's also inviting us to join the grand adventure he's on. Maybe the greatest question we can ask ourselves—and maybe the hardest to answer—is "What is the meaning of life?" But another way to ask that question is "What is my role in the adventure God has invited everyone into?" Let's explore that question by taking a much closer look at that same clip from *The Return of the King*.

Video Clip

Once again, play the "Coming Home" scene from *The Return of the King,* the last film of *The Lord of the Rings* trilogy. Cue up the extended edition of the film to Side B 1:40:10, and play the clip until 1:41:41. Ask everyone to pay close attention to the characters in this scene and try to discern what's going on inside them.

After the clip, someone should ask: *(2 minutes)*

- Now, after we've watched this clip more closely, what do you notice about these guys?

- The adventure seems to have changed them—how?

If no one else mentions them, the study leader can talk about the "Hobbit Insights" on page 18.

Someone should say: Let's compare this scene and the grand adventure it represents to a scene from the Bible. *The Lord of the Rings* could be a parable of Matthew 10, where Jesus tells his disciples about the grand adventure he's sending them on. This is where he moves them off the sidelines and into the game.

Trio Talk: *(10 minutes)* Get with two others to form a trio. Together, scan Matthew 10, where Jesus prepares to send out his disciples two by two. He wants them to spread the good news about the Messiah, heal people, and cast out demons. But Jesus won't be going with the disciples this time; they'll be on their own. In your trio, pick out every instruction and expectation Jesus gives them for their adventure. List them here:

1.

2.

3.

4.

5.

6.

7.

8.

9.

10.

Gather again as a group, and have a spokesperson from each trio read the trio's list. Each trio should share things on its list only if the things haven't been mentioned already by previous trios.

After the trios answer, the study leader can talk about the "Adventure Prep From Jesus" points on page 19 if no one else has mentioned them.

Someone should ask: *(3 minutes)*

- What are the similarities and differences between the adventure the disciples are about to undertake and the one the hobbits have completed?

Someone should say: Just like the hobbits, when the disciples return from their adventure, something profound has changed in them. The Apostle John records a scene that happens after he and the others have returned from their adventure. Jesus tells his disciples and the gathered crowds that "unless you eat the flesh of the Son of Man and drink his blood, you have no life in you."

That bizarre statement is enough to drive everyone away; the crowds of thousands leave. Finally, only the 12 disciples are left.

And Jesus asks them, "You do not want to leave too, do you?" (John 6:67). But the disciples' adventure has cemented their relationship. They've experienced what it means to live a life that's dependent on Jesus for everything. So Peter answers, basically, "Nope, where else would we go? We're committed to living in the adventure you've plunged us into."

Someone should ask: *(2 minutes)*

- What are some similarities and differences between this scene from the Bible and the scene we watched with the four hobbits from *The Return of the King*?

Someone should say: Steve Jobs, the legendary co-founder of Apple Computers, successfully recruited PepsiCo president John Sculley to take over as CEO of Apple by asking him, "Do you want to spend the rest of your life selling sugared water, or do you want a chance to change the world?"

We have to ask ourselves, "Do we want to look like the villagers in this scene who get pretty excited about a big pumpkin, or do we want a look in our eyes like the hobbits have? Do we want a look that says we're part of something way bigger than ourselves, something significant, something deep in the heart of God?"

But what is deep in the heart of God? What would we be doing if we joined Jesus on his adventure? I think we get a pretty clear picture in Luke 4, when Jesus announces the start of his ministry.

Someone should read aloud Luke 4:18-19: "The Spirit of the Lord is on me, because he has anointed me to preach good news to the poor. He has sent me to proclaim freedom for the prisoners and recovery of sight for the blind, to release the oppressed, to proclaim the year of the Lord's favor."

Someone should ask: *(3 minutes)*
Jesus is telling everyone why he came. He's describing what he intends to do on his grand adventure. If we were to join him, what exactly would we be doing? What would it look like for us to

- proclaim freedom for the prisoners?

- help people who are blind recover their sight?

- release people who are oppressed?

- proclaim the year of the Lord's favor (a time when debts were canceled and people were freed from oppression)?

After the group answers the questions, someone should say: Dave Freeman co-wrote the book *100 Things to Do Before You Die*. Not long ago, he fell at his home and died at age 47. If we're looking to find our role in God's big adventure, we could read Freeman's book (he didn't complete his own list). Or we could go see the film *The Bucket List*, the story of two men who create lists of things they want to do before they "kick the bucket." Or we could ask Jesus for our own personal bucket lists.

Someone should say: *(5 minutes)*
Put everything down and relax your body. *(Pause.)* Take a deep breath. *(Pause.)* Now pray, asking God to help you hear—to sense—his voice and his guidance. *(Pause.)*

Now ask God the following two questions, and wait for the answers. If you sense something from God, write it in the space below.

Two Questions

1. God, what's one adventurous thing you want me to do before I die?

2. God, what's one adventurous thing you want me to do this week?

Close by asking people who'd like to share what they wrote to do so. If one of the "this week" ideas will work for the whole group, decide how you can all do it together. Then have someone offer a prayer of thanks to God.

HOBBIT INSIGHTS

- The adventure created a kind of gravity—or weight—to the characters.

- The adventure seemed to make the hobbits feel like outsiders. They felt somehow different from the people around them.

- They've left behind "childish things" and are acting like men.

- In the trilogy's first film, before the hobbits are swept into this adventure, Sam loves Rosie (the girl in the scene) but doesn't have the courage to tell her. Now, after living a grand adventure, he knows he has something to offer her.

ADVENTURE PREP FROM JESUS

1. Jesus has a *specific* mission for his disciples.

2. Jesus wants them to "freely give" what they have to others.

3. Jesus wants his disciples to feel utterly dependent. He doesn't want them to count on themselves but to trust God to take care of them.

4. Jesus promises that other people will aid them in their adventure. And for those people who don't provide aid, it won't go well for them.

5. Jesus says the disciples will be at the mercy of people around them.

6. Jesus says they'll be betrayed and opposed, so they shouldn't be surprised. He's been treated harshly already, and he promises the disciples they'll be treated even more harshly.

7. He tells them they'll be misunderstood and even hated.

8. He reminds the disciples that God greatly values them, no matter what their circumstances or what others say about them.

9. Jesus tells them their job is to bring light where there's darkness.

10. He asks the disciples to lose their life for him.

EXTRA-MILE IDEAS

- Plan a *Lord of the Rings* Lock-In—Show all three films back to back during an overnighter or a retreat. Use the films as the central focus of your time together. After each film, do a short Bible study that's targeted to that film's message:

1. *The Fellowship of the Ring*—Do a Bible study on the role of community in our adventures.

2. *The Two Towers*—Do a Bible study on the spiritual battle all Christians are part of and what our role in it is.

3. *The Return of the King*—Do a Bible study on the qualities we need to persevere in our adventures.

- Study the book *Do Hard Things* by Alex and Brett Harris—Use the book's online study guide (at therebelution.com) to go through the book together.

Tough Thing   N°. 2

DENY YOURSELF

Study Prep

When Jesus told his disciples (and us) to deny ourselves, take up our cross, and follow him (Luke 9:23), he took a great risk. The risk was that we would respond to his invitation with a sort of dread—a kind of earnest commitment to kill our desires, hopes, and dreams and replace them with drudgery. Well, he was really inviting us to "take the road less traveled," a road that's full of adventure and wonder and purpose and meaning. But it all starts with a tough word: *deny*.

Note on Supplies

You'll need to cue up the trailer for the film *The Chronicles of Narnia: The Lion, the Witch and the Wardrobe*. You can find it on the film's DVD, in the "Special Features" section. It's also on YouTube at youtube.com/watch?v=ALd8nIyWCgs (or you can type in "The Lion, the Witch and the Wardrobe Trailer" into YouTube's search box). You'll also need a bunch of pennies and quarters (the same number of each, and enough so that half your group can have one of each).

Video Clip ◎

Play the theatrical trailer for the film *The Lion, the Witch and the Wardrobe*.

After the clip, someone should say: The house has many rooms and many doors. But only one door leads to another world. This setup to *The Lion, the Witch and the Wardrobe* is a lot like Robert Frost's famous poem "The Road Not Taken." It goes like this:

> Two roads diverged in a yellow wood,
> And sorry I could not travel both
> And be one traveler, long I stood
> And looked down one as far as I could
> To where it bent in the undergrowth;
>
> Then took the other, as just as fair,
> And having perhaps the better claim,
> Because it was grassy and wanted wear;
> Though as for that the passing there
> Had worn them really about the same,
>
> And both that morning equally lay
> In leaves no step had trodden black.
> Oh, I kept the first for another day!
> Yet knowing how way leads on to way,
> I doubted if I should ever come back.
>
> I shall be telling this with a sigh
> Somewhere ages and ages hence:
> Two roads diverged in a wood, and I—
> I took the one less traveled by,
> And that has made all the difference.

In the Narnia story, the younger sister, Lucy, certainly took the road less traveled...or the door less opened. Instead of getting scared or skeptical, she pushed through the door into a world of adventure.

Pair Talk: Everyone should get with a partner now. *(Pause.)* Now take a couple of minutes each to talk about a time you took a road less traveled in your life. It could be a place, a decision, or an action. The person wearing the most blue should go first.

Someone should ask: *(3 minutes)*

- In general, what motivated you to take your road less traveled?

- Is the road less traveled typically easier or harder than the alternative? Explain.

Someone should say: Jesus talked about a road less traveled, too. It's a narrow road that's accessible only through a small gate.

Someone should read aloud (from Matthew 7:13-14): Jesus says, "Enter through the narrow gate. For wide is the gate and broad is the road that leads to destruction, and many enter through it. But small is the gate and narrow the road that leads to life, and only a few find it."

And later (in John 10:7-10) he says, "I tell you the truth, I am the gate for the sheep. All who ever came before me were thieves and robbers, but the sheep did not listen to them. I am the gate; whoever enters through me will be saved. He will come in and go out, and find pasture. The thief comes only to steal and kill and destroy; I have come that they may have life, and have it to the full."

Foursome Talk: *(4 minutes)* Now join with another pair to form a foursome. *(Pause.)* Then discuss these questions:

- What exactly does Jesus mean when he talks about the small gate and the narrow road? Why are few people on it?

- Why does Jesus call himself the "gate," and what is he trying to say to us?

After four minutes, gather back together with the group.

Someone should say: Let's hear back from everyone. What are some of your insights?

After a few responses, someone should say: Like the path into Narnia and the decision Robert Frost talks about in his poem, Jesus is asking us to open the gate, or door, "less opened" and walk the path "less traveled." In this study, we'll explore the less-traveled path Jesus is inviting us to explore—the path of denying the way we choose for ourselves and taking the path Jesus has invited us onto.

In *The Lion, the Witch and the Wardrobe*, the Beavers try to describe Aslan (the character who's like Jesus) to the children who walk through the door into Narnia. They say he's good but not safe. The same is true of the narrow way that Jesus is inviting us to take. It's good but not safe—because Jesus is good but not safe, and he is the "way." Walking the narrow way might make us feel off balance and out of control, two things we don't like very much.

A Spun Experience: *(5 minutes)* Get back with your original partner. The person who has the longest arms should be the first "spun" person. That person should close his or her eyes and quickly spin around in place five complete revolutions. Then the "spun" person's partner should ask:

- What's making you feel "spun" right now in your life? I mean, where and how do you feel sort of dizzy, unbalanced, or out of control?

After this, the partners should switch roles and repeat everything.

Then everyone should gather back together.

Someone should ask the whole group:

- What are the pros and cons of feeling off balance in your life?
- How does the thought of denying yourself make you feel off balance and out of control?

Someone should say: So often, Jesus said and did things that made people feel off balance. In how he lived and what he said, Jesus seemed to relish asking people to do impossible things, such as denying themselves. For example, there's the story of the rich young ruler.

Someone should read aloud Luke 18:18-23:
A certain ruler asked him, "Good teacher, what must I do to inherit eternal life?"

"Why do you call me good?" Jesus answered. "No one is good—except God alone. You know the commandments: 'Do not commit adultery, do not murder, do not steal, do not give false testimony, honor your father and mother.'"

"All these I have kept since I was a boy," he said.

When Jesus heard this, he said to him, "You still lack one thing. Sell everything you have and give to the poor, and you will have treasure in heaven. Then come, follow me."

When he heard this, he became very sad, because he was a man of great wealth.

Someone should ask: *(10 minutes)*

- Why did Jesus respond this way to the young man?

- Why did Jesus tell him to sell everything he had and follow him?

- What exactly was Jesus planning to give this guy if he would deny himself?

- If you were in this guy's shoes, what reasons—pro and con—would you consider when you were deciding how to answer Jesus?

A Penny-and-a-Quarter Experience: Whoever gathered the pennies and quarters before the study should take them out and give one penny or one quarter to each person. Form pairs, with one Penny Person and one Quarter Person. In each pair, the Penny Person should form a fist around the penny and hold the fist out in front of him or her, with fingers toward the floor. The other person in each pair should put the quarter on his or her open palm, about five inches below the partner's closed fist. The game is played like this:

- The Penny Person in each pair should try to quickly snatch his or her partner's quarter without losing the penny.

- The Quarter Person in each pair must keep his or her hand open until the Penny Person tries to snatch the quarter. Then the Quarter Person can quickly close his or her hand.

Pairs should try this several times. (It's usually quite hard to do without letting go of the penny.)

Someone should ask: *(5 minutes)*

- What comparisons can you make between this experience and the story of the rich young ruler?

- What are examples from your own life of giving up something "lesser" to get something "greater"?

Someone should say: What if, instead of thinking about "denying ourselves" as a downer, we see it as a road less traveled, a path that leads us to better things than we ever could have imagined for our lives? Let's spend a few minutes in total quiet right now, asking God this question:

- God, what's one way you'd like me to take the road less traveled right now in my life; what's one way I can deny myself so I can follow your path instead?

Right here in your book, journal what you sense God telling you:

After a few minutes, close in prayer. Take the opportunity to thank God publicly for what he's shown you now.

EXTRA-MILE IDEAS

Take a Real "Road Less Traveled"—Sometime in the near future, move your regular group meeting to an unusual location. It could be either a different room or a completely different place. While in your new location, take 30 minutes to brainstorm together one way you could "change the world" for at least one person. Figure out how to do it. Then do it.

Plan a Fast Alternative Day—As a group, choose one day when you'll all fast from one meal. Together, brainstorm lots of ideas for what you can do in place of eating that meal. Come up with things that offer God's grace to people around you. It could be prayer time, an act of kindness, or even writing encouraging postcards to people who need them. You choose what to do. Then commit to doing it.

Plan a "Deny Yourself" Fundraiser—Together as a group, decide on one thing that each of you can cut out of your life for one week or one month. It should be something that will save you money over that time, such as coffee, texting, or going out to eat. Collect the money you save, and give it to a ministry that helps people who've had the basics of life, like food and freedom, forcibly denied. You can contact Compassion International (compassion.com) or World Vision (worldvision.org) for ideas.

Tough Thing   N⁰ 3

PASSIONATELY PURSUE

Study Prep

It's in God's nature to pursue us. First John 4:19 says, "We love because he first loved us." And Matthew 18:12 says, "What do you think? If a man owns a hundred sheep, and one of them wanders away, will he not leave the ninety-nine on the hills and go to look for the one that wandered off?"

Pursuit is central to God's character. In fact, we wouldn't be followers of Christ if God wasn't, by nature, a pursuer. And because we're created in God's image, we were created to pursue others. But the sad fact is that we're often not very good at it. Pursuing people well is tough. In this study, we'll explore together the thrill of pursuing people with all our hearts, just as God does with us.

Note on Supplies

You'll need a DVD of the film *The Horse Whisperer*.

Someone should say: The Bible is a collection of true stories with God as the central character. What is God doing in these stories? He's most often pursuing people, trying to show them how much he loves them, and inviting them into a relationship with him. Sometimes Jesus goes to great lengths to pursue us, such as when he knocked Saul to the ground in Acts 9, temporarily blinding him.

Today, are we as interested in people and their stories as God is? Well, yes, as long as those people are celebrities. *American Idol* host Ryan Seacrest once told *Entertainment Weekly*, "Our culture is obsessed with the people we see on television and watch in the movies." We're fascinated by the stories of celebrities, but we're often not all that curious about the most fascinating, stunning, and compelling people on earth—"regular" people like you and me. God is the greatest author ever, and he's writing our stories!

Someone should say: In the film *The Horse Whisperer*, Robert Redford plays Tom Booker, a cowboy renowned for his ability to work with difficult horses. In the film's pivotal scene, Tom is trying to make a breakthrough with Pilgrim, a horse badly injured after a truck slams into him. The accident almost kills Pilgrim's owner and rider, 14-year-old Grace. Doctors must amputate her leg, and she's been in a deep depression ever since.

Meanwhile, Pilgrim is disfigured and emotionally unstable. The veterinarians advise Grace's mom to destroy the horse, but the mom refuses. So the horse lives in limbo. He's too injured, angry, and afraid to be ridden but not so damaged that he can't eat, sleep, and...exist. So Grace and her mom load the horse in a trailer and take off to Montana to convince Tom to help Pilgrim. In this scene, Tom is working with Pilgrim for the first time.

Video Clip ◎

Show the scene of Tom Booker working with Pilgrim for the first time, from the film *The Horse Whisperer*. Cue up the DVD to 56:23, and stop it at 1:02:37.

Someone should ask: *(5 minutes)*

- Why does Pilgrim act the way he does?

- What's powerful about the way Tom pursues the horse? Why is it powerful?

- When, if ever, have you been pursued like this?

- Describe a time when you pursued someone like this; what did that look like?

Someone should say: This is a story of breakthrough. Pilgrim is a perfect symbol for many of the people around us. We're wounded, afraid, and lonely. We don't easily let others "in" to really touch our souls. And who has the time and patience to persist in pursuing people who won't let us in? We need help if we're going to pursue people the way God does.

The legendary talk-show interviewer Larry King, known for his ability to pursue people well, once wrote an article outlining how he does it. Let's learn from four of King's strategies.

Someone should say: The first strategy is "Be curious." King says, "If you're sincerely curious, more people want to talk than don't."

Someone should ask: *(3 minutes)*

- What does "sincere curiosity" look like?

- How do you know when someone is sincerely curious about you?

- What do sincerely curious people do differently from the rest of us?

Someone should say: The second strategy is "Follow through." The great singer Frank Sinatra was tight-lipped with most interviewers but not with Larry King. Sinatra once told him, "I feel when I'm with you, there's no camera or microphone. You make that disappear because I know that you're listening to what I'm saying."

Another way to say this is "Be passionately present." We can be passionately present to people by asking more, and better, questions of them. Too often we don't know how to ask good questions, or we give up too soon. So we never really get to know someone well.

Asking "The Next Question": *(3 minutes)* Pair up with someone. *(Pause.)* The person with the longest fingernails gets to be the Questioner, the person asking the questions. The topic of this conversation is "Should teenagers be allowed to choose whatever they want to watch or listen to, or should parents get to set boundaries on those choices?" The Questioner should ask as many follow-up questions as you can. Don't worry if your partner can't answer right away. Just wait, or ask the question in another way. But keep asking questions until three minutes are up! Don't stop!

After three minutes, gather back together.

Someone should ask: *(1 minute)*

- What was challenging about this exercise?

Someone should say: Pursuing people is like exercising your muscles. The more and better questions you ask, the better chance you have of knowing that person. The third Larry King strategy is called "Focus." He says, "Look behind the voice and into what [the person is] saying." Really, he's encouraging us to think of ourselves as detectives trying to unravel a mystery, and the mystery is the person in front of us. People give us clues to their "real selves" all the time. They tell us things that show something deeper about themselves, but we're not always paying attention. For example, sometimes people use stronger-than-normal words (*hate* instead of *don't like,* for example) to express opinions. Those clues can often tell you something deeper about who that person really is.

Following the Clues: Close your eyes, and think back to a conversation you had with someone during today's study. Then ask God to show you a clue that person showed you about himself or herself— something that revealed his or her real self.

After a minute or so, someone should ask: *(2 minutes)*

- Who thought of something? Can you share it?

Someone should say: If we're focusing and paying better attention to people, we'll pick up clues about who they really are. The fourth Larry King strategy is "Avoid yes-and-no questions." These are questions that can be answered with a simple yes or no. We'll learn how to pursue others better if we ask questions that focus on why, what, and how, not questions that can be answered yes or no.

Yes-and-No No More: *(5 minutes)*
Get back with a partner. This time, the person with the longest eyelashes gets to be the Questioner. Your goal is to discover how your partner became the person he or she is. But you can't ask any questions that can be answered with a simple yes or no—again, no yes-or-no questions. You have two minutes; then you should switch roles.

After four or five minutes, someone should ask: *(2 minutes)*

- Was this exercise easier or harder than you expected, and why?

Someone should say: Fear keeps us from really pursuing others, doesn't it? That's another reason we need God's help so much. And practice helps. Larry King has done more than 10,000 on-air interviews, so he's had lots of practice. Let's challenge ourselves to be the best people-pursuers we know.

Close in prayer, asking God for the courage and determination to pursue others the way he pursues us.

EXTRA-MILE IDEAS

A Larry King-athon—Record an episode of *Larry King Live,* and watch it together as a group. Take notes as you watch, listing ways King seems effective at pursuing others. Then, as a group, come up with five new "pursuit strategies" based on what you observe.

Peer Power—Plug people into good "pursuit" roles through peer-to-peer ministry opportunities. Youth pastor Mike Bradley, writing in Group Magazine, offers these possibilities:

1. Leaders of small groups—These groups can meet weekly for fellowship, prayer, and Bible study.

2. "Disciplers" or "spiritual friends"—Disciplers should be able to effectively communicate the basics of the faith. And they should provide a "sounding board" to new converts when they face tough decisions or temptations.

3. Peer counselors—In our fragmented and performance-oriented culture, young people often need someone they can talk to. Teenagers make great counselors after they've received basic training that includes listening skills. Group Publishing created a wonderful resource for basic training that's now out of print, but you can order it by searching on abebooks.com. Just type *Training Teenagers for Peer Ministry* by Barbara Varenhorst into the search box.

4. Visitation team members—It's important that visitors to your group have someone to connect with soon after they've visited. So train a team of teenagers to do it.

5. Worship leaders or team members—You probably have kids in your group who love to worship, sing, or play music. They're prime candidates to lead or participate in a worship team at group meetings.

Tough Thing No. 4

BECOME A DISCIPLE (PART 1)

Study Prep

Ever wonder how much of the Christian life is really about trying harder? Is that *really* what Jesus had in mind—sacrificing his life to win us the chance to...try harder? A life of following Jesus is often called discipleship. It references the disciples, who gave their lives to follow Jesus. If people who grow in discipleship are the ones who try the hardest, it's no wonder more people aren't living as disciples of Jesus.

But what if life and discipleship are about more than trying harder? What if the really tough thing isn't trying harder but yielding ourselves to Jesus more often and more deeply? In this study, we'll compare the "we try harder" approach to following Christ to the well-known stories of two women who anointed Jesus with perfume.

Note on Supplies

For each person, you'll need a scrap of paper with a little dab of perfume on it. You'll also need to copy the discussion guides at the end of this study and pile them separately on two sides of your meeting area. Bring a cross of some kind to this study, and be prepared to play a quiet instrumental song for the closing time.

Someone should ask: Who knows the company slogan for Avis Rent A Car? *(The answer is at the bottom of this page, so tell everyone there's no peeking!)*

Pair Talk: *(3 minutes)*
Get together with a partner. *(Pause.)* Now discuss this question. The person who got the most sleep last night gets to go first:

- Is Avis' slogan—"We try harder"—something that God always honors in people? Why or why not?

After a few minutes, ask everyone to gather together so pairs can share highlights from their discussions.

Someone should say: Trying harder is a deeply held value for most of us. How many times have you heard your parents encourage you to try harder? When it comes to following Jesus, trying harder represents the road most traveled. We're pretty convinced that trying harder is the answer to most challenges in our lives, including the challenge of following Jesus. We're "Avis people" in the church.

Someone should ask: *(1 minute)*

- What "try harder" messages have you heard in the church?

After everyone has a chance to respond, someone should say: The Bible contains prominent examples of people trying harder. Some are positive examples, and some aren't. For example, the Pharisees—the same people who plotted to kill Jesus—made a name for themselves by trying harder. They made a big show of how well they followed God's law, and they even made up lots of new laws just so they'd have more to follow. When Jesus saw how the Pharisees were using "trying harder" to justify themselves and lord it over others, he lashed out at them by calling them "snakes," "whitewashed tombs," and even "sons of hell" (Matthew 23).

Of course, there's nothing evil about trying harder. The alternative seems like denial or laziness or arrogance. But the Bible gives

What is the company slogan of Avis Rent A Car? **"We try harder."**

us the example of another path, the narrow road less traveled. It tells of two desperate women to whom Jesus gave extraordinary honor. *(Pass out little pieces of paper with perfume on them.)* As we read these two stories from Eugene Peterson's paraphrase of the Bible, *The Message*, let's close our eyes and listen deeply. Keep the paper close to your nose, and breathe it in as you listen.

Have someone read aloud Luke 7:36-50 from *The Message*: The first story happens pretty early in Jesus' ministry, when the Pharisees were still trying to figure out what they thought of him. Let's listen to the story of "Jesus Anointed by a Sinful Woman":

One of the Pharisees asked him over for a meal. He went to the Pharisee's house and sat down at the dinner table. Just then a woman of the village, the town harlot, having learned that Jesus was a guest in the home of the Pharisee, came with a bottle of very expensive perfume and stood at his feet, weeping, raining tears on his feet. Letting down her hair, she dried his feet, kissed them, and anointed them with the perfume. When the Pharisee who had invited him saw this, he said to himself, "If this man was the prophet I thought he was, he would have known what kind of woman this is who is falling all over him."

Jesus said to him, "Simon, I have something to tell you."

"Oh? Tell me."

"Two men were in debt to a banker. One owed five hundred silver pieces, the other fifty. Neither of them could pay up, and so the banker canceled both debts. Which of the two would be more grateful?"

Simon answered, "I suppose the one who was forgiven the most."

"That's right," said Jesus. Then turning to the woman, but speaking to Simon, he said, "Do you see this woman? I came to your home; you provided no water for my feet, but she rained tears on my feet and dried them with her hair. You gave me no greeting, but from the time I arrived she hasn't quit kissing my feet. You provided nothing for freshening up, but she has soothed my feet with perfume. Impressive, isn't it? She was forgiven many, many sins, and so she is very, very grateful. If the forgiveness is minimal, the gratitude is minimal."

Then he spoke to her: "I forgive your sins."

That set the dinner guests talking behind his back: "Who does he think he is, forgiving sins!"

He ignored them and said to the woman, "Your faith has saved you. Go in peace."

Then have someone read aloud Matthew 26:6-13 from *The Message*: The second story happens near the end of Jesus' ministry, when his attention was squarely on the cross. Keep your perfumed paper in front of your nose while we listen to the story of "Jesus Anointed at Bethany":

When Jesus was at Bethany, a guest of Simon the Leper, a woman came up to him as he was eating dinner and anointed him with a bottle of very expensive perfume. When the disciples saw what was happening, they were furious. "That's criminal! This could have been sold for a lot and the money handed out to the poor."

When Jesus realized what was going on, he intervened. "Why are you giving this woman a hard time? She has just done something wonderfully significant for me. You will have the poor with you every day for the rest of your lives, but not me. When she poured this perfume on my body, what she really did was anoint me for burial. You can be sure that wherever in the whole world the Message is preached, what she has just done is going to be remembered and admired."

Someone should say: *(10 minutes)*
Now let's explore the two women in these stories. This side of the room is for Story 1, and the other side of the room is for Story 2. You and your partner from before will go to opposite sides of the room. So get together right now, decide which side of the room you'll go to, and then go there. *(Pause.)*

Once you've moved to your side of the room, find a new partner, grab one of the papers piled on your side, and discuss the questions. *(Pause for a three-minute discussion.)*

Now come back to your original partner, and share what you learned about your story. Discuss common themes or connections between the two stories. *(Pause for a three-minute discussion.)*

Gather back together.

Someone should ask: *(5 minutes)*
Now let's map the narrow road less traveled in these stories.

- How do these women's actions contrast with the "we try harder" approach we've generally embraced in the church?

After everyone has had a chance to answer, someone should say: Now let's spend a couple of minutes in silence. Close your eyes, and ask God this question: "What do you *really* want from me?" When you think you might have sensed an answer from God, bring your scented piece of paper up to the cross and lay it at its foot. You can linger if you'd like or return to your seat. I'll play a song that will help us embrace this time. After you've had time to be quiet, I'll close in prayer.

EXTRA-MILE IDEAS

Slogan-ize—Because "We try harder" isn't the best message for discipleship, have your group brainstorm a slogan that better fits your discipleship mission. For example, you could choose "We smell better" to reference this study's perfume stories. Make buttons out of the slogan (get a button maker at buttonbiz.com), and ask people to wear the buttons on their coats or attach them to their backpacks as a way to start conversations about your discipleship mission.

Get to Know Me—Often, the reason we think trying harder is the way to grow in our relationship with Christ is that we haven't gotten to know him very well. Most of us are highly motivated to grow in relationship with the people we love the most. And we love those people because we know them well. One great way to fuel your knowledge of Jesus is to spend more time getting to know him. After your group finishes this study, consider doing the 10-week study *In Pursuit of Jesus: Stepping Off the Beaten Path*. You can get it at youthministry.com or at a Christian bookstore.

Mural-ize—Cover one wall of your meeting room with newsprint, or, if you meet in a home, just use one poster-size piece of paper. Title it "Great Things About Jesus." At the end of every meeting, add new things to the poster or mural. Use words, pictures, and even stuff that's taped to the paper. Keep going until the poster or mural is completely full. Use the finished piece of art as a reminder of who Jesus really is and what he really does.

"Jesus Anointed by a Sinful Woman"

Luke 7:36-50

Discussion Questions

• Put yourself in the shoes of this woman. What was motivating her to do what she did?

• What was she communicating to Jesus?

• Jesus seemed to love what she did for him—why?

• Can you think of a time when you approached Jesus in a similar way? Share that story with your partner.

"Jesus Anointed at Bethany"

Matthew 26:6-13

Discussion Questions

• Put yourself in the shoes of this woman; what was motivating her to do what she did?

• What was she communicating to Jesus?

• Jesus seemed to love what she did—why?

• Can you think of a time when you approached Jesus in a similar way? Share that story with your partner.

Tough Thing N⁰. 5

BECOME A DISCIPLE (PART 2)

Study Prep

Jesus never forced himself on anyone. He invited; he didn't demand. But it's clear that Jesus was looking for people who wanted more—more of him. As it turns out, a lot of people preferred to have less of Jesus. In the end, the people who decided they wanted more of him were called his disciples.

That's still true today. Each of us has to decide whether we want more or less of Jesus. One of the tough things about life is that our choices really do affect us in profound ways. Whether we want more or less of Jesus, it will influence the way we live. In this study, we'll compare the "I want less" and "I want more" approaches to following Christ.

Note on Supplies

You'll need little pieces of bread and little pieces of meat (steak is perfect, but sliced roast beef from a deli will work, too), enough for each person to have one or the other. Put each piece of food in a little Dixie cup. You'll be giving each person a cup containing either a piece of bread or a piece of meat. Also, you'll need a DVD of the film *Dead Poets Society*. And you'll need to be prepared to play a worship song as your closing.

Someone should say: Feeling full right now? Got any room left in that tummy? You're going to need a little bit of space in there.

Wonder Bread or Steak?: Everyone but the leader of this exercise should get with a partner and then close his or her eyes. Then the leader should give each person a Dixie cup containing either a piece of bread or a piece of meat. People should keep their eyes closed. Tell partners to simultaneously eat what's in their cups. Then, with their eyes still closed, people should describe to their partners (in great detail) what they're eating—the texture, taste, density, and satisfaction of eating it. The bread person should go first. People should say anything they can think of to describe what they're eating. Get specific!

After both partners have shared, get back together as a group.

Someone should ask: *(2 minutes)*

- What are some of the significant differences you discovered between eating bread and eating meat?

Someone should say: Jesus used bread and meat to help people understand what it means to follow him, to be his disciple. Essentially, he says he'll give us bread to eat, but he longs for us to want something more substantial—*meat*—instead.

In John 6, after Jesus fed a huge crowd with just five loaves of bread and two fish, he tries to explain to the people following him that the "Wonder Bread" they'd just eaten is nothing compared to "the living bread that came down from heaven" that he represents (verse 51). He asks them to consume him as if he were living bread.

Jesus explains this concept over and over, finally getting blunt after the people start arguing with him about it: "How can this man give us his flesh to eat?" they ask (verse 52). Let's go back to that story to remind ourselves how Jesus responds to them.

Have someone read aloud John 6:53-56, 66-67 from *The Message*:

> But Jesus didn't give an inch. "Only insofar as you eat and drink flesh and blood, the flesh and blood of the Son of Man, do you have life within you. The one who brings a hearty appetite to this eating and drinking has eternal life and will be fit and ready for the Final Day. My flesh is real food and my blood is real drink. By eating my flesh and drinking my blood

you enter into me and I into you. In the same way that the fully alive Father sent me here and I live because of him, so the one who makes a meal of me lives because of me. This is the Bread from heaven. Your ancestors ate bread, and later died. Whoever eats this Bread will live always."

After this a lot of his disciples left. They no longer wanted to be associated with him. Then Jesus gave the Twelve their chance: "Do you also want to leave?"

Have someone ask: *(2 minutes)*

- What does Jesus mean when he tells his disciples they must eat his flesh and drink his blood?

After everyone has a chance to respond, continue by having someone read aloud John 6:68-69 from *The Message*:

Peter replied, "Master, to whom would we go? You have the words of real life, eternal life. We've already committed ourselves, confident that you are the Holy One of God."

Have someone ask: *(3 minutes)*

- What motivated the people who left Jesus to give up on him?

- What motivated the disciples who stayed to hang in there?

Someone should say: Remember from our second study that the remaining 12 disciples are *really* choosing the narrow road less traveled. Those who remain are saying, in effect, "I'm willing to want more of you, Jesus." Those who left were saying, in effect, "I was OK with this arrangement. You give me bread, and I listen to what you say. But now you're asking too much!"

People on the road less traveled seem to fundamentally want more of Jesus. People on the well-worn road seem to want Jesus on their own terms, in measured, manageable portions. Aren't we taught to not want anything *too much*? Haven't we learned that wanting more can be dangerous?

Let's watch a scene from the film *Dead Poets Society* that explores these questions. In this scene, the students at a pretty uptight boarding school for boys meet their new teacher for the first time.

Video Clip ◎

Show the scene from *Dead Poets Society* where John Keating (played by Robin Williams) encourages students to rip out the introductory pages from their poetry books. Cue the DVD to 21:00, and end it at 26:45.

After the clip is over, everyone should get with a partner.

Partners should discuss these questions: *(4 minutes)*

- What was Keating trying to communicate to the boys?

- What connections can you make between this scene and the Bible passages we just read?

Someone should say: Maybe Keating was trying to teach these by-the-book students how to *want more*—how to pursue something with all their hearts. Peter's response to Jesus was, essentially, "I don't know exactly what you're asking me to do, but I know I want you, and I'm not going anywhere." The big question is this: How do we get to a place where we want more of Jesus, where he asks us to eat his flesh and drink his blood, and we say, "I'm not exactly sure what you mean, but I'm in!"?

Someone should ask: *(3 minutes)*

- What are some things we've done—or could do—to fuel our hunger for more of Jesus?

Someone should list the responses so everyone can see them.

Someone should say: *(3 minutes)* Let's spend a few minutes in silence, looking at this list and simply asking God this question:

- Which of these things, if any, are you asking me to do, God?

After a few minutes, ask everyone to keep their eyes closed as you play a worship song.

After the song, ask if anyone wants to share what they sense God asking them to do. As a group, affirm and support what people share.

EXTRA-MILE IDEAS

Do a "Best Friends of Jesus" Study—Assign everyone in your group one chapter from one of the gospels (Matthew, Mark, Luke, or John). Have each person scan his or her chapter to compile a list of Jesus' friends, people he liked to hang out with. Gather together to compile one master list of Jesus' friends, and then look for common threads among these people. To do that, ask questions such as "What motivated these people to befriend Jesus? What was their social status in the culture? What did they want from Jesus? What were they hoping to give Jesus?"

After you've compiled your common threads, ask, "How many of these common threads do we share right now? What would have to be different in our lives in order for us to share more of these common threads?"

Barbecue Parables—Plan a group barbecue at someone's home. Plan a menu that includes meat, vegetables, fruit, and dessert. After the meal, gather to talk about each aspect of it.

For the meat, ask, "What do we like most about eating meat? How is it different from eating salad, for instance? What aspect of our relationship with Jesus is like eating meat, and why?"

For the vegetables, ask, "What do we like most about eating vegetables? How is it different from eating dessert, for instance? What aspect of our relationship with Jesus is like eating vegetables, and why?"

For the fruit, ask, "What do we like most about eating fruit? How is it different from eating vegetables, for instance? What aspect of our relationship with Jesus is like eating fruit?"

For the dessert, ask, "What do we like most about eating dessert? How is it different from eating meat, for instance?

EXTRA-MILE IDEAS (continued)

What aspect of our relationship with Jesus is like eating dessert?"

After you finish discussing each menu item, talk about how discipleship is like eating a well-rounded meal, with dessert at the end.

Start a Facebook Page for Your Go-Deeper Group—Form a group of teenagers who are interested in "diving deeper" with Jesus. Then set up a Facebook page for your group. Participants can use the page to share their own "go deeper" ideas, ask each other questions, post music that fuels a deeper relationship with Jesus, post photos of the group's activities, and so on.

Tough Thing № 6

DEFEND YOUR FAITH

Study Prep

Defend sounds like there's a war going on. And biblically there is. The Bible says we have an enemy, a "thief" who "comes only to steal and kill and destroy" (John 10:10). His name, of course, is Satan. And our enemy's go-to weapon should be no surprise: He likes to lie, all the time. In the end, if we don't grow in our ability to counter our enemy's lies, we lose ground. Lives are on the line here.

So defending our faith isn't about winning arguments with people. It's about upholding the truth in a world that's brimming with lies. And when people hear the truth, they find freedom from the prison they're living in. Jesus told us that "the truth will set you free" (John 8:32). Know anyone who needs freedom? There's nothing tougher than a freedom fighter, and when you defend your faith well, that's exactly what you are.

Note on Supplies

You'll need a glass container (a jar or large drinking glass, for example) filled with marbles, M&M's candies, pennies, or any small things you have around the house or church. Choose someone to bring the container to the study, and make sure that person knows how many items are in the jar (that person should keep the number a secret). For every two people, you'll also need a brown-paper lunch bag with an unusual object inside (tiny stuffed animals, figurines, toys, and so on).

Guess How Many?—Have the person who brought the filled container display it for the whole group.

Someone should ask:

- How many [marbles, M&M's, pennies, etc.] do you think are in this jar?

Write each person's guess, and then celebrate the person who guessed closest to the actual number.

Then someone should ask: *(1 minute)*

- What's your favorite song?

Write each person's favorite song right here in your book:

Then ask: *(2 minutes)*

- Which one of these songs is the best one?

After everyone has a chance to answer, someone should say: How is asking how many marbles are in a jar different from asking which song is the best? What about this question...

Ask: *(2 minutes)*

- Is Jesus the Son of God, the one-and-only path to salvation?

Follow up by asking: *(2 minutes)*

- Is this last question more like the question about how many marbles are in the container or more like the question about which song is best? Explain.

Pair Talk: *(3 minutes)* Our culture often confuses tolerance with relativism. Get with a partner now, and come up with a definition for both words, *tolerance* and *relativism*.

After a few minutes, get back together as a group and share your answers. Look for common definitions, and as a group decide on one definition for each word. Each person should write the final definitions right here:

Tolerance:

Relativism:

Someone should ask: *(2 minutes)*
Let's make this even more personal.

- Was our discussion about final definitions fueled more by tolerance or relativism? Explain.

After everyone has a chance to respond, someone should say: Some people (including some here) think the question about Jesus being the only way to salvation is more like the question about the best song. We'd say Jesus is our "favorite," but we can't say he's the "best" because others have their own favorites. Tolerance, many people believe, requires that we account for others' "favorite" paths to salvation. This kind of tolerance can lead to relativism, which essentially says that Jesus is our truth but he's not other people's truth.

But Jesus says he's *the* "way and the truth and the life" (John 14:6). The way the Bible answers this question is more like the answer to our first question about the container. There are a certain number of somethings in there. It's a "hard" truth. And this is exactly why apologetics, or the ability to defend your faith, is a tough thing. Apologetics is sort of a lost art for Christians today. Why? Let's get together with a partner right now to explore the answer to that question.

Brown Bag, Brown Bag: Each pair should now get one brown-paper lunch bag with an object inside it. The top of each bag should be folded over so no one can see inside. One person in the pair should be the Teacher and the other should be the Learner. The Teacher gets to put his or her hand inside the bag and touch the object for one minute, all the while trying to describe the object to the Learner. The Teacher isn't allowed to use the name of the object to describe it.

After one minute, someone should ask *only* the Learners: What is your object?

Then someone should ask the Teachers: What is your object?

Now someone should say: Now all the Teachers should pull out their object to see what it really is.

Someone should ask: *(3 minutes)*
Let's say that your object represents our faith in Jesus.

- How were the challenges in this activity like the challenges we face in defending our faith to others?

- What are some reasons we often struggle to defend our faith in today's culture?

Someone should say: It's hard to describe something that we ourselves are fuzzy about. So let's explore three "starter" ways we can learn to defend our faith.

What's Cool With Jesus? *(7 minutes)* Get with a partner right now. Start reading in one of the gospels—Matthew, Mark, Luke, and John—and see how quickly you can come up with a list of "10 Things Jesus Thinks Are Cool." Write them in the space below.

After five minutes, get back together and compare lists. Come up with a master list of "Things Jesus Thinks Are Cool." Write them in the space below.

Problem Time: *(7 minutes)* Now switch partners and, together, start reading one of the gospels again. Look for at least one "problem" or "hard question" you can ask based on what you've read. For example, "Why did Jesus treat the beggar woman in Matthew 15 so harshly?"

After five minutes, gather again and share your questions. Decide together who you can ask to tackle these questions for you—your pastor, youth pastor, or another Bible-wise person. Ask a volunteer to either send the questions to that person and ask for a reply, or invite the person to your next gathering to answer the questions.

Top Five Truths: *(5 minutes)* As a group, you have just five minutes to agree on the five most important truths of the Christian faith. Discuss these questions:

- What makes these truths the most important?

- What makes these truths different from other beliefs and religions?

Someone should say: Jesus told us that he was sending the Holy Spirit—the "Teacher"—to us so we could learn much more about him. Let's invite the Holy Spirit to take us to graduate school. Our response can be to revisit what Jesus thinks is cool, to seek answers to hard questions, and to continue focusing on our five important truths. As we grow in our ability to describe our faith, we'll grow more confident defending it.

Close in prayer.

EXTRA-MILE IDEAS

If your group is interested in exploring more ways to defend your faith, consider these:

Use a "Guest Panel" to Answer Teenagers' Questions— Pennsylvania youth pastor TJ Reid says:

> We've been using an [apologetics] idea that's working very well. Every month we invite a panel of four church members who are Bible-literate to answer our kids' faith questions. Our group members get thoughtful responses about the truths of their faith, and they get to interact with adults who are living their faith and able to answer kids' questions on the spot (the same way they're often challenged). The change in our young people has been amazing. They're far more confident in their faith and more eager to reach out to their friends.

Do a Book Study—Use one of these three resources to wrestle with core biblical truths: *The Case for Christ*, Student Edition, by Lee Strobel (Zondervan); *Jesus Among Other Gods*, Youth Edition, by Ravi Zacharias (Thomas Nelson); and *The New Evidence That Demands a Verdict*, by Josh McDowell (Thomas Nelson).

Create a Summer "Seals Training" Group—Advertise this as a group for "the few, the proud..." Use summer's flexible schedule to compare Christian beliefs with those of other faiths, to practice telling the gospel story, to explore biblical truths through feature films, or to do a "harmony of the gospels" study.

Tie a "Mystery Question" Into One of Your Five Most Important Truths—Use the last 10 minutes of each week's meeting time to challenge teams to answer the question first, with biblical backup. For example, "True or false: The Bible teaches that although the best way to heaven is through faith in Christ, there are other ways that work as well."

Every Few Months, Ask a Non-Christian to Tell His or Her Story to Your Group—After the person leaves, discuss what you learned about the way non-Christians see the world. Discuss how those ways are similar to and different from a biblical worldview.

Tough Thing No. 7

SHARE YOUR FAITH

Study Prep

As children, we're all taught that sharing is one of the nicest things we can do for others. That applies to almost everything in life, with the notable exception of *sharing our faith*. A lot of people think it isn't nice at all for others to share their faith with them. It feels pushy, judgmental, and overbearing.

Sharing our faith is a tough thing, but maybe that's because we've lost the whole concept of *sharing*. Sharing means extending something good to people so they also can enjoy its benefits. What could be better than the promise of a life with Jesus, hidden "in the shadow of his hand" (Isaiah 49:2)?

In the case of Jesus and his mission of redemption, the benefit we experience is his rescue of us. Why wouldn't we want to share that with people we care about?

Note on Supplies

You'll need a DVD of the film *The Guardian*. And it would be helpful if everyone who has a cell phone brought it to this study.

Intro: Show the rescue scene from the beginning of the film *The Guardian*. Cue up the DVD to 1:06, and stop it at 4:40.

Someone should say: This scene is from the film *The Guardian*, which is about the Coast Guard's rescue swimmers. The movie's tagline is "When lives are on the line, sacrifice everything." In a Coast Guard with 30,000 members, there are only about 300 rescue swimmers. It's considered some of the toughest training in the military. These people must perform rescues in some of the most terrifying circumstances you can imagine, like the scene we just watched.

Trio Discussion: *(3 minutes)* Get with two other people to form a trio. Then tell about a time you were rescued from something or someone. After three minutes or so, gather back together as a group.

Someone should ask: *(5 minutes)*

- What emotions did you feel toward the person who rescued you?

- Do you feel embarrassed or self-conscious telling others about the person who rescued you? Why or why not?

Someone should say: Many of us are who we are because we've been rescued by Jesus. He rescued us from the penalty of our sins and from a life apart from him. Of course, maybe some of us haven't yet experienced that feeling of rescue. But one thing is profoundly true: Rescue is at the heart of God. Even so, we often interfere with God's rescue plans for our lives.

Someone should ask: *(5 minutes)*

- In the scene we just watched, what was different about the way the man and the woman responded to their rescuer?

- What are all the factors that made the rescue difficult?

- How do these factors compare to the difficulties God faces when trying to rescue us from our sins?

- How do these factors compare to the difficulties we have in helping others accept the rescue that Jesus offers?

Someone should say: It's a strange thought, but it often isn't easy to convince drowning people to accept their rescue. In the case of the rescue that Jesus offers, people sometimes don't think they're "drowning," so why would they need to be rescued? Or sometimes they trust only themselves to get out of their mess. Or sometimes they're so overwhelmed by their circumstances that they just give up or give in. When we share our faith with other people, we're really just hoping they'll also trust their life to the Great Rescuer, Jesus.

Let's learn from a 15-year-old guy named Chad who's discovered a lot about helping others trust Jesus as their rescuer. Awhile back, Group Magazine asked Chad to offer his advice on how teenagers can share their faith because he has a great track record of developing friendships with kids who haven't committed their lives to Christ.

Listen First: When Jesus reached out to the hated tax collector Zacchaeus in Luke 19, the first thing he did was make time to listen to his story. Jesus said, "Zacchaeus, come down immediately. I must stay at your house today" (verse 5).

Chad says that "listening first" is the foundation for evangelism, and it's fun! Let's practice right now.

Get with a partner. To get started, ask your partner the following question (you'll each have two minutes for this):

- What are your beliefs about God, and how did you arrive at those beliefs?

Ask lots of follow-up questions, if necessary. After each person has had two minutes to answer, get back together, and have everyone briefly summarize his or her partner's answers for the whole group.

Someone should ask: *(3 minutes)*

- In addition to the question we just discussed, what are three more great "opener" questions we could ask non-Christians to help us focus on listening?

Write the three questions the group comes up with here:

1.

2.

3.

Resist Getting Defensive: *(5 minutes)* Chad learned, over time, that the biggest turn-off for non-Christians is when Christians get defensive about their beliefs. Instead, he found ways to connect with the doubts, arguments, and resistance that people have to faith in Christ.

Get back with your partner, and choose who will play the role of a Christian and who will play the role of a non-Christian in your conversation. Then have the "non-Christian" person choose one of these typical attacks on Christianity:

- Christians are so hypocritical.

- I already believe in God. Christians are so arrogant they think they're the only ones who are "in" with God.

- Religions are the source of a lot of violence and abuse in the world.

- Christians are so narrow-minded. I want to have fun in life!

- Most of the Christians I've met are mean and condescending.

The "Christian" partner should use one of the three questions we just came up with to start a conversation. The "non-Christian" partner should respond as if he or she really believed that typical attack. The "Christian" partner should practice nondefensive responses, such as asking clarifying questions, finding something in the argument he or she agrees with, or probing how the person came to those beliefs about Christianity. The goal is to make a relational connection. *(Of course, this might feel a little awkward at first. That's OK, just have fun with it.)*

Just Do It! *(5 minutes)* Now it's time to take the road less traveled and experience a five-minute adventure. Everyone who has a cell phone should take it out. Now think of one friend who either isn't a follower of Christ or isn't very serious about following Christ.

In just a moment, call that person and start a conversation using the skills and questions we've just learned. It sounds tough, but it's not as awkward or hard as it sounds.

Just say something such as "Hey, I'm in the middle of a little project, and I'm wondering if you have five minutes to chat."

Then review the opening questions we came up with, and remember the conversational skills we just practiced. After a few minutes, you can thank your friend and end the call.

For those of you who don't have a phone or can't reach your friend, you can listen to someone who's having a conversation and offer feedback. Go!

After five minutes, or when everyone is finished calling, gather to debrief the experience.

Someone should ask: *(5 minutes)*

- If you made a call, what happened, and how did it feel?

- If you couldn't call, what feedback do you have for those who did?

Someone should say: Here are two final bits of advice from Chad:

1. First, learn what "God questions" other people have, instead of assuming you know what they are. Just ask.

2. Don't be afraid to say, "I don't know" when you're conversing with a non-Christian. Instead of covering for yourself or making up an answer, just say something such as "That's a good point. I've never really thought of that before. I'll have to think about it before we talk again."

Let's close by praying for our friends who haven't yet embraced Jesus as their rescuer.

EXTRA-MILE IDEAS

Q-and-A Opportunities—Go to a mall with a video camera, and ask teenagers these questions on camera: "If you could ask God any question and be guaranteed an answer, what would it be? What's the biggest problem you have with people who say they're Christians? What's the biggest reason you don't go to church more often?" After you film people's responses, explain that you're Christians who are curious about people's responses to these big questions. Look for opportunities to extend your conversation and share your faith.

Cliqueing It—As a group, identify as many cliques in your local schools as you can. Brainstorm what these groups like to do and where they like to hang out. Then pick one of the cliques and plan an outreach event that involves those people and their interests. Repeat this process for every clique. Then choose one idea and try it.

RAK Teams—With your kids, brainstorm one Radical Act of Kindness you can implement every month. Or form a RAK team whose purpose is to counteract meanness and stinginess as often as possible. Or in every newsletter you send to kids, suggest at least one everyday Radical Act of Kindness. Surprising people with kindness wins you the right to connect with them.

Tough Thing No. 8

ACT SHREWDLY

Study Prep

If you called a friend shrewd, would that person still be your friend? For a lot of people, the answer would be no. Most people don't say things such as "I just love my best friend—she is the shrewdest person I know!" Uh...thanks.

But here's the funny thing about Jesus. He's always embracing and promoting surprising concepts:

- The first will be the last.

- The least will be the greatest.

- Mosaic law was made to serve us; we're not supposed to serve the law.

Add one more surprising thing to this list: Jesus believes that shrewdness is crucial, and he wishes more of us had it. You'll see what I mean as you dive into this study. Learning how to be more shrewd in life is definitely tough, but it's also one of the most exciting, satisfying aspects of a growing relationship with Jesus.

Note on Supplies

You'll need to write the group's ideas on a large piece of paper so everyone can see them.

Defining *Shrewd*: Get with a partner and discuss these questions:

- How would you define the word *shrewd*?

- Why do we most often see this word as more negative than positive?

Gather as a group, and have each pair summarize its discussion. As a group, come up with a shared definition of *shrewd*, and write it in the space below so everyone can see it.

Someone should say: Our definition of *shrewd* is important because, as it turns out, Jesus thinks shrewdness is a crucial skill for us to learn. He showed us that when he told his disciples the parable of the shrewd manager in Luke 16.

In the story, a rich man accuses his business manager of not handling his money well, of wasting his resources. The manager is lazy and proud, and he's afraid he'll actually have to work hard to earn a living. So he cuts deals with all the rich man's creditors, slashing what they owe before he gets fired. That way, he reasons, these people will take him in after he loses his job. When the rich man finds out what his good-for-nothing manager has done, he praises him! He's happy because the guy exercised shrewdness to get what he needed. Jesus then comments on the story by saying:

> The master commended the dishonest manager because he had acted shrewdly. For the people of this world are more shrewd in dealing with their own kind than are the people of the light (Luke 16:8).

This parable is perplexing, even disturbing.

Someone should ask: *(5 minutes)*

- Why would Jesus praise the lazy, proud manager in this story?

- Why are "the people of this world" more shrewd than Christians are?

- Why does Jesus want Christians to be more shrewd?

Someone should say: Later on, Jesus again highlights the importance of shrewdness. Just before he sends his disciples out two by two to preach the gospel, heal the sick, and cast out demons—the first time they'll be ministering without him—he gives them two instructions: "I am sending you out like sheep among wolves. Therefore be as shrewd as snakes and as innocent as doves" (Matthew 10:16).

The disciples—and we—are supposed to be both innocent and shrewd. The word *shrewd* here is the same word used in the Bible to describe Satan. Jesus is saying that one of the two most important things we can learn, as his disciples, is shrewdness. This is the same kind of shrewdness Satan exhibits but not for the same purpose. Satan wants to steal and kill and destroy with his shrewdness. Jesus wants us to bring life, light, and redemption with our shrewdness.

Someone should ask: *(3 minutes)*

- What are examples of Jesus using his shrewdness to bring life, light, and redemption?

- What are examples from your own life, or from stories you've heard, of people using shrewdness to bring life, light, and redemption?

Someone should say: Earlier, we came up with our own definition of *shrewd*. Here's another practical, and neutral, definition of the word: "Shrewdness means understanding how things work." So if you understand how things work, you can bring good leverage to situations. That's how the shrewd manager in Jesus' parable avoided becoming homeless and destitute. Good leverage means you understand how you can use your influence to bring about a desired outcome. Now we're going to get into Shrewd Teams of two people each so we can study how things work.

How Things Work: *(10 minutes)*
After you've found a partner, choose something from the list below (or come up with your own "thing" to study) and spend 10 minutes discovering how it works. You can use whatever means you have available. Call a friend or a parent, use the Internet if you have it,

physically examine the thing—whatever works for you. Just make sure you have a detailed understanding of how it works within the next 10 minutes. You'll be asked to report to the group what you've discovered.

How Does This Work?

- How does carpet work?

- How does a light bulb work?

- How does a car engine work?

- How does a pen or marker work?

- How does a washing machine work?

- How does an iPod work?

- How does a DVD player work?

- How are fabrics made?

- How do you train a wild animal?

- How does a telephone work?

- How does a good marriage work?

- How does a "best friendship" work?

- How does an airplane fly?

After 10 minutes, come back together. A few of the Shrewd Teams should share what they learned.

Someone should say: Now let's apply the "understanding how things work" process to something real in our lives—something God would like us to move toward in shrewdness. Let's focus on the impact of gossip in your school. Gossip happens in every school. Actually, it happens wherever many people are gathered regularly. And gossip can destroy people. Here's what the Apostle James says about the power of the tongue in James 3:3-6:

When we put bits into the mouths of horses to make them obey us, we can turn the whole animal. Or take ships as an example. Although they are so large and are driven by strong winds, they are steered by a very small rudder wherever the pilot wants to go. Likewise the tongue is a small part of the body, but it makes great boasts. Consider what a great forest is set on fire by a small spark. The tongue also is a fire, a world of evil among the parts of the body. It corrupts the whole person, sets the whole course of his life on fire, and is itself set on fire by hell.

Here's our challenge as a group. Let's use our powers of shrewdness to come up with a plan to stop the destructive impact of gossip in our schools.

The Gossip Challenge: *(15 minutes)* Together as a group, explore how gossip works. Then come up with a shrewd plan to counteract it. Questions you may want to consider include:

- How does gossip start?

- How is gossip spread?

- How does gossip become destructive?

- Although everyone knows gossip is wrong, why do we all still do it?

- Is gossip all bad?

- What kind of person usually is involved in gossip, and what kind of person usually isn't involved in gossip?

- What's more powerful than the tongue, and why?

- What would have to happen for gossip to "die on the vine"?

Remember to work fast. You have only 10 minutes for this challenge.

At the end of 10 minutes, come up with a plan you all agree on to stop the destructive impact of gossip in your schools. Then figure out how you'll implement that plan and how you'll gauge your results. Remember that shrewdness is understanding how things work then leveraging that knowledge for good. Before you begin, someone should pray, asking God for wisdom on how to be shrewd about gossip. Go!

Closing prayer: After you've figured out your shrewd plan to stop gossip, close by thanking God for his wisdom and asking him for help in carrying out your plan.

EXTRA-MILE IDEAS

Community Shrewdness—As a group, brainstorm a "Top 10 List of Community Problems." These can be physical problems, social problems, spiritual problems...anything. Look at your list, and decide together which problem seems to be the biggest one facing your community. Then break into smaller teams to brainstorm "how things work" in your community, relative to the problem you've chosen. Come back together, and share what you've come up with. Then create a plan for shrewdly addressing that community problem. Then do it! By the way, this would be a great time to contact the media and get them interested in your project. Spread the shrewdness!

Study Satan's Shrewdness—The Bible often describes Satan as shrewd. So do a Bible study that focuses on how, why, and when Satan is shrewd. Then take what you've learned and transform it. Figure out how to take what Satan intends for evil and turn it to good, just as Joseph did. He'd been thrown in a pit and left for dead but later rose to power in Egypt and ultimately saved all of Israel from famine. Joseph told his brothers, "You intended to harm me, but God intended it for good to accomplish what is now being done, the saving of many lives" (Genesis 50:20). To get you started, here are a couple of Scripture passages about Satan's shrewdness: Genesis 3:1-7; and Job 1:6-12, 2:1-7.

Tough Thing N°· 9

LOVE YOUR ENEMIES

Study Prep

Here's a perfect example of a "tough thing," right from Jesus' mouth: "You have heard that it was said, 'Love your neighbor and hate your enemy.' But I tell you: Love your enemies and pray for those who persecute you, that you may be sons of your Father in heaven. He causes his sun to rise on the evil and the good, and sends rain on the righteous and the unrighteous" (Matthew 5:43-45).

This little statement is tough on so many levels. First, Jesus says, "You have heard that it was said...." Essentially, he's saying that the "truth" you've always heard isn't quite right. He's about to tell us how it really is. Then Jesus matter-of-factly tells us to do what seems impossible: to love people whose intentions toward us are evil.

In so many of the tough things that are central to a life of following Christ, our own resources just aren't enough. It's as if God has told us to do things we can't possibly do on our own. "Impossible" is really beyond tough. But "impossible" just might be an invitation to relationship.

Note on Supplies

You'll need a DVD of the film *Les Misérables*—the 1998 version starring Liam Neeson.

Someone should say: To start, let's each find a partner (preferably of the same gender), and stand up facing each other. The person with the most hair on his or her head is 1, and your partner is 2. In each pair, partner 1 should extend an open hand, palm down, toward partner 2. Partner 2 should extend an open hand, palm up, an inch or so underneath partner 1's hand.

The goal of this game is for partner 2 to try to quickly slap the top of partner 2's hand before he or she can jerk it away. We'll play this for 30 seconds. After each attempt, partner 2 should put his or her hand back under partner 1's hand and try again until I call time. If you're a 2, see how many times you can slap your partner's hand in 30 seconds. If you're a 1, see if you can avoid getting slapped altogether.

Play Slap-Hand: Partners should keep playing for 30 seconds, until the leader says to stop.

Someone should say: OK, now switch roles. All 2s should extend an open hand, palm down, in front of them. And all 1s should extend an open hand, palm up, just under the partner's hand. Again, we'll play for 30 seconds.

Play Slap-Hand Again: Partners should keep playing for 30 seconds, until the leader says to stop.

Someone should ask: *(3 minutes)*

- What feelings or emotions did you have as we played this game?

- How might this game promote feelings of revenge? Explain.

- There's a popular psychological saying that goes "Hurt people hurt people"—why do you suppose that's true?

Someone should say: People hurt us, sometimes every day. Some-times it's unintentional, but sometimes they're trying to hurt us. Those people usually become our enemies. And it's really hard to resist the temptation to hurt them back. Maybe one of the toughest things Jesus ever told us to do is love our enemies. Let's hear the whole context surrounding what he was telling us.

Someone should read aloud Matthew 5:38-48:

> You have heard that it was said, "Eye for eye, and tooth for tooth." But I tell you, Do not resist an evil person. If someone strikes you on the right cheek, turn to him the other also. And if someone wants to sue you and take your tunic, let him have your cloak as well. If someone forces you to go one mile, go with him two miles. Give to the one who asks you, and do not turn away from the one who wants to borrow from you.
>
> You have heard that it was said, "Love your neighbor and hate your enemy." But I tell you: Love your enemies and pray for those who persecute you, that you may be sons of your Father in heaven. He causes his sun to rise on the evil and the good, and sends rain on the righteous and the unrighteous. If you love those who love you, what reward will you get? Are not even the tax collectors doing that? And if you greet only your brothers, what are you doing more than others? Do not even pagans do that? Be perfect, therefore, as your heavenly Father is perfect.

Someone should ask: *(7 minutes)*

- Why would Jesus ask us to do something that seems so hard?

- Why would Jesus seem to contradict the Old Testament standard for dealing with enemies—"an eye for an eye"?

- If you actually followed Jesus' command, how would that change your life?

- If all Christians actually followed Jesus' command, what are some positive and negative things that might happen in the world?

Someone should say: The 1998 film version of Victor Hugo's classic novel *Les Misérables* opens with ex-convict Jean Valjean trudging toward Digne, his hometown. He was just released from a French hard-labor prison, where he spent 19 backbreaking, soul-crushing years for stealing a loaf of bread for his hungry family. Valjean has to report to his parole officer in Digne within four days, or he'll be sent back to prison. He's angry, bitter, and desperate. He stops for the night in an unnamed village—exhausted, alone, and hope-less—and curls up on a hard bench to snatch a few hours of sleep. In the scene we're about to watch, you'll see an old woman ap-proach and tell Valjean he can't sleep on the bench. Let's watch.

Video Clip

Cue up the DVD of the 1998 version of *Les Misérables* to 2:54, and stop it at 9:52.

After the clip, someone should ask: *(15 minutes)*

- At the beginning of this scene, how does the old woman know that Valjean hasn't yet knocked on the bishop's door?

- How would you describe the bishop in this scene?

- How would you describe the environment of the bishop's home?

- How do you explain the bishop's behavior toward Jean Valjean, both before and after their violent encounter?

- On the surface, the bishop's reaction to Valjean after the police capture him seems almost foolish and naïve. Why would the bishop take such a chance on Valjean?

- How would you expect Valjean to respond to the bishop's actions and words for the long term?

- What are some ways the bishop is like Jesus, and what are some ways Valjean is like us?

- If everyone in this group acted a little more like the bishop in this scene, what impact might that have on our community?

Someone should say: Let's revisit what Jesus told us about our relationships with our enemies. Specifically, he told us to love our enemies and pray for people who persecute us. Get with a partner right now. We'll explore what it would look like if we actually did what Jesus said, rather than just talked about it.

Loving and Praying for Enemies: *(10 minutes)* Without using names, share with your partner something about a person you consider to be a current or former enemy.

After each person has shared, look at the list below of "responses to enemies" taken from Jesus' instructions to his disciples:

- Don't argue for your rights with an enemy.

- Respond with overwhelming grace to an enemy.

- If an enemy tries to take from you, give that person something greater instead.

- If an enemy tries to force you to do something, act extravagantly on behalf of that person.

- Help meet your enemy's needs.

Now each of you should choose one of these broad responses to enemies to try as an experiment with the person you just mentioned. Together, brainstorm ideas about how each of you could carry out your experiment. Help each other come up with a strategy to love your enemy based on one of these "Jesus" responses.

After you've each come up with a plan, spend some time praying:

- Ask God to give you the strength and spiritual "fuel" you need to follow through on your plan.

- Ask God how you should pray for your enemy. Then do it.

Someone should say: If all of us follow through on our plans, we'll have miraculous stories to tell. It doesn't even matter how our enemies respond. The fact that we've lived out Jesus' seemingly impossible command is worth celebrating. To seal our "enemy lovers" pledge to God and each other, let's get in a tight circle. *(Pause.)* Now

EXTRA-MILE IDEAS

The Enemies List—When the Watergate scandal came to light, one of the most attention-getting discoveries was President Richard Nixon's "Enemies List." It was a list of his major political opponents and was part of a campaign officially known as the "Political Enemies Project." The purpose, as described by the White House Counsel's Office, was to harm Nixon's political enemies by IRS tax audits and by manipulating "grant availability, federal contracts, litigation, prosecution, etc."

What if you created an "Enemies List," but for totally different reasons? Create a list that includes the names of people who are, or who have been, your enemies. Keep the list in your Bible or hidden somewhere so others won't see it. Then:

1. Every day, pray for one person on your Enemies List. Pray that God would bless that person and draw him or her to God.

2. Every month, do something to respond to an enemy in "the opposite spirit." It could be simple or more involved, but do something on behalf of the person that's completely opposite from how the person has treated you.

Get to Know Your Enemy—The celebrated author Studs Terkel spent his whole life writing about working people, exploring their stories as if they were treasure chests. In one story, he relates how offended he was when he watched the film

let's each put our right hand in the middle of the circle, one on top of the other. *(Pause.)* Will someone please close us in prayer?

At the end of the prayer, everyone should say amen to break the huddle.

Five Easy Pieces, in which a grumpy waitress is mocked and humiliated after she refuses to serve something not on the menu.

Here's what Terkel said about that scene: "What are we told of this nasty woman? Was it afternoon? Was it near the end of a long day for her? And how were her varicose veins? And what happened behind those swinging doors? Did she and the chef have words? And why was she waiting on tables? Was her old man sick? Did he run off? Was her daughter in trouble? And how many Bufferins did she just take? Perhaps she was indeed a Nogood Girlo. We'll never know."

Terkel is saying that we often respond to our enemies with no knowledge at all about their lives. And knowledge about their lives could help us respond to them in love instead of revenge. So pick someone who's now, or has been, your enemy, and figure out a way to answer these questions:

- What is this person's home life like?

- What hurts, pains, or wounds has this person experienced?

- What is missing from this person's life?

- What has fueled this person's attitude toward me?

- God has compassion for all of us; when he thinks of this person, what is he feeling compassion for?

Tough Thing N⁰· 10

DO JUSTICE

Study Prep

Everyone's interested in justice. Sound like an overstatement? Well, think of the number of times you've said "that's not fair" in your life. A lot. You've probably struggled with some issue of justice even today.

So it's no surprise that the Bible gives a great deal of attention to justice. The word is used 134 times in Scripture, and justice is at the core of both Old Testament law and the gospel of Christ. That's because God himself is just; he hates injustice.

And God has made it clear that we're to live our lives honoring what is just. Micah 6:8 says, "He has showed you, O man, what is good. And what does the Lord require of you? To act justly and to love mercy and to walk humbly with your God." The trouble is, acting justly isn't as easy as it sounds. We're motivated to stick up for our own "rights," but what about the rights of others?

Note on Supplies

You'll need to cut up a length of ribbon into smaller ribbons—enough for about one-third of your group to have one small ribbon—and gather the same number of stick pins. You'll also need a DVD of the film *The Lord of the Rings: The Return of the King.*

Ribbon Wearers: Whoever's leading this study should have the supply of ribbons and stick pins. The leader should secretly decide on a specific reason to give certain people a ribbon (and a stick pin). Think of your own criteria for why you're giving only one-third of the people in your group a ribbon. Your reason could be based on color of clothing, color of hair, kind of shoes, height, or something completely random. Don't tell anyone your criteria. Ask each person who receives a ribbon to use the stick pin to attach the ribbon on their clothing somewhere.

Someone should say: I've decided that everyone who's wearing a ribbon right now should get the most comfortable seats in the room. So everyone who *isn't* wearing a ribbon, will you please make sure that everyone who *is* wearing a ribbon is sitting in the most comfortable seats? If all the seats are the same, find some way to make the ribbon wearers more comfortable in their seats. We'll wait until that happens. *(Pause.)*

Someone should ask: *(10 minutes)*

- If you have a ribbon on, how did your selection as a ribbon wearer affect you?

- If you don't have a ribbon on, how did that affect you?

- What criteria do you think was used to give away ribbons?

- Was this little exercise fair? Why or why not?

- How much does fairness depend on the criteria you use? Explain.

- How much does your opinion of what is and isn't fair depend on your opinion of the person setting the criteria? Explain.

- What should happen now, if anything, to make things fair? Explain.

After the group answers these questions, the leader should reveal his or her criteria for giving away ribbons.

Then someone should ask: *(2 minutes)*

- Now that you know the criteria, does that change whether you think this exercise was fair? Why or why not?

Someone should say: Of course, this is a relatively unimportant exercise in fairness. But it taps into much more serious questions about justice. Let's brainstorm some of the most important "justice issues" facing people in the world right now. Let's see how many we can come up with.

Justice Around the World: As justice issues come up, list them in your book:

Someone should say: In Isaiah 56:1, the prophet says, "This is what the Lord says: 'Maintain justice and do what is right, for my salvation is close at hand and my righteousness will soon be revealed.'" To explore what maintaining justice and doing what's right look like in a practical situation, get with two others to form a trio.

Do the Right Thing: *(10 minutes)* As a trio, look at your list of justice issues around the world and pick one to focus on. Then answer these questions together:

- What is the central issue of justice involved in this particular situation?

- Who's responsible for the injustice?

- Who's in a position to correct the injustice?

- In this situation, what are the barriers to establishing justice?

- What would have to happen to bring justice to this situation?

- How likely is it that the people involved in this situation can receive justice? Explain.

As a trio, come up with one thing you could do to nudge this situation toward justice.

Someone should say: It's tough to actually think of making a difference in an unjust situation, rather than just talking about the injustice. The great American author, activist, and lecturer Helen Keller—the first deaf and blind person to graduate from college—said, "I am only one, but still I am one. I cannot do everything, but still I can do something; and because I cannot do everything, I will not refuse to do something that I can do."

When we bring justice into any situation, we get to participate in the glory of God. God is caught up in the rescue of those he loves. That's the glory of his life. Many of Jesus' parables were stories of rescuing lost things or people. And Jesus describes his life's purpose this way: "For the Son of Man came to seek and to save what was lost" (Luke 19:10). So how do we join Jesus in his work of maintaining justice and doing right in the world?

We can learn something from the film *The Lord of the Rings: The Return of the King* that will help us answer that question. In the scene we're going to watch, the leader of the forces of good, the soon-to-be-king Aragorn, leaves his warriors and saddles his horse for a trip down Dimholt Road. He's going to visit an army of dead people who "live" as ghosts under a mountain. His mission is to give them a chance to repent for betraying a previous king by joining his army in the war against the forces of evil. The elf Legolas and the dwarf Gimli insist on going with Aragorn. They arrive at the dark entrance to the mountain, having ridden through a spooky, silent valley. Let's watch what happens then.

Video Clip

Show the scene from *The Lord of the Rings: The Return of the King* where Aragorn and his two companions go through the mouth of a cave and into the "home" of an army of dead people. Cue up the scene at 1:46:48, and end it at 1:49:15.

After the clip, someone should ask: *(5 minutes)*

- How is this scene a metaphor for pursuing justice?

- What can we learn from this scene about why so few people pursue justice in the world?

- What can we learn from this scene about why some people do pursue justice in the world?

Going Into the Cave: *(2 minutes)* Right now, in your own life, what's the "cave" of justice that God is asking you to enter? Take two minutes to silently ask God this question. If you sense clarity or an answer, write it below.

Someone should say: To go into the cave with people means to bring light to darkness, to participate fully in God's great mission. It's what it means to bring freedom, not just to the person but to everyone who can benefit from what that person has to give.

Let's stand now and close our eyes. *(Pause.)* If you sensed something from God and wrote it in your book, would you be willing to share what you wrote with the whole group? As each person speaks, the rest of us will respond by saying, "To God's glory, and in his power, go into the cave!" I'll close in prayer at the end.

EXTRA-MILE IDEAS

Invite a Justice Guest—Ask someone from a justice-focused ministry or organization to come to your group or church to talk about justice opportunities around the world and in your back yard. You can request a speaker from International Justice Mission at ijim.org, Run your cursor over the Resources button, and then click on IJM Speakers to fill out a request form.

Or go to the Not For Sale campaign's website at notforsalecampaign.org. Run your cursor over the "Who Are We?" button, and then click on the "State Directors" link to contact someone in your area. Or Google "anti-slavery," along with your town, to see if a local organization can provide you with a speaker.

Join the "Be the Change" Movement—Zach Hunter started his work as an abolitionist—an antislavery activist—when he was just 14. He wrote a book titled *Be the Change* to get more young people involved in the movement. Your group can get involved by participating in the "Loose Change to Loosen Chains" campaign. Learn about it on Zach's MySpace page at myspace.com/lc2lc.

NOTES